THE magical nordic TAROT

BE INSPIRED BY NORDIC LEGENDS AND EXPLORE YOUR PAST, PRESENT, AND FUTURE

ILLUSTRATIONS BY
hannah davies

jayne wallace

CICO BOOKS
LONDON NEW YORK

ACKNOWLEDGMENTS

Many thanks to Hannah Davies for her wonderful illustrations and to Tracey Emin for the beautiful Charity card artwork. Thanks to publisher Cindy Richards and the great team at CICO Books who have helped bring my vision to life. Thanks also to my brilliant team at Psychic Sisters, Selfridges, my fiancé, Leigh Ryan, my agent, Chelsey Fox, and Naz Alibagi, who helped shape my words.

Published in 2020 by CICO Books
An imprint of Ryland Peters & Small Ltd
20-21 Jockey's Fields   341 E 116th St
London WC1R 4BW   New York, NY 10029

www.rylandpeters.com

10 9 8 7 6

Text © Jayne Wallace 2020
Design © CICO Books 2020
Illustrations © Hannah Davies 2020, apart from Charity card (page 35) © Tracey Emin

The author's moral rights have been asserted. All rights reserved. No part of this publication may be reproduced, stored in a retrieval system, or transmitted in any form or by any means, electronic, mechanical, photocopying, or otherwise, without the prior permission of the publisher.

A CIP catalog record for this book is available from the Library of Congress and the British Library.

ISBN: 978-1-78249-886-5

Printed in China

Senior Designer: Emily Breen
Commissioning editor: Kristine Pidkameny
Senior editor: Carmel Edmonds
Art director: Sally Powell
Head of production: Patricia Harrington
Publishing manager: Penny Craig
Publisher: Cindy Richards

Contents

INTRODUCTION 4
Getting to Know Your Cards 5
Beginning a Reading 5
Finishing a Reading 6

THE SPREADS 6
One-card Reading 6
Past, Present, Future 7
The Nordic Compass 8
The Horseshoe 9
The Light Within 10
The Clock 11

THE MAJOR ARCANA 12
0 The Fool 13
I The Magician 14
II The High Priestess 15
III The Empress 16
IV The Emperor 17
V The Hierophant 18
VI The Lovers 19
VII The Chariot 20
VIII Justice 21
IX The Hermit 22
X The Wheel of Fortune 23
XI Strength 24
XII The Hanged Man 25
XIII Death 26
XIV Temperance 27
XV The Devil 28
XVI The Tower 29
XVII The Star 30
XVIII The Moon 31
XIX The Sun 32
XX Judgment 33
XXI The World 34
XXII Charity 35

THE MINOR ARCANA 36
Suit of Pentacles 37
Suit of Cups 44
Suit of Wands 51
Suit of Swords 58

INTRODUCTION

With a rich and magical history, Nordic myths have held a special place in my heart since I was a little girl and first heard about the Northern Lights. Enchanted by their beauty, I learned their history and soon found myself falling in love with everything connected to Nordic legends and beliefs. Many years later, when I was able to see the lights for myself during a trip to Iceland, my love for Nordic mythology grew even stronger, and as I watched the Northern Lights dancing in the sky, I knew I wanted to create a Nordic-inspired Tarot deck one day—and now I have.

This Tarot deck combines traditional Tarot imagery and meanings with Nordic mythology, incorporating some of my favorite legends, which include stories about powerful spirit animals and the gods and goddesses and their magical powers.

Also included in this deck is a specially commissioned additional Major Arcana card designed by my client and friend, Tracey Emin. Tracey shares my love of Tarot and in particular how we connect with our spirit animals, which can be seen in the card she has drawn, XXII Charity (see page 35). The card's keyword is "generosity," which reflects Tracey's generosity of spirit in creating the card for me.

Whether you're at the start of your Tarot journey or have been reading for many years, the cards in this deck are designed to help you deepen your understanding of the cards' meanings and enhance your Tarot-reading skills. The cards can be used to provide an empowering affirmation for the day or for readings, whether quick or in-depth.

I've also included advice on how to connect with your deck, tips on how to read the cards, and a few spreads to help you get started. Remember, the information in this book is only for guidance, so find your own routine and see what works for you.

If you're new to Tarot, try reading for yourself first with the One-card Reading (see page 6). Pay attention to the colors, keyword, and imagery on each card, and take note of your intuitive responses before looking up the meaning on pages 13-35. By writing down any patterns you notice, you can develop your own interpretations of the cards, and what they represent to you.

Once you're feeling more confident, practice reading for others, and use their feedback to enrich your understanding of the cards. Remember, practice makes perfect—so practice, practice, and practice some more!

GETTING TO KNOW YOUR CARDS

Before reading with this deck, you need to connect with its energy, and form a sacred bond with your cards. You can do this by going through the deck and touching each card, or by sleeping with the deck under your pillow for a week. Alternatively, you could start by picking a card to focus on each day, and familiarizing yourself with each one individually. Once you've connected with your deck, you can start reading with your cards.

BEGINNING A READING

Begin by finding a quiet space, and creating a relaxing atmosphere by lighting some candles or burning some incense. Choose a spread you feel drawn to from pages 7-11, or one of your own, and hold the deck with both hands.

Shuffle the cards, and start to breathe slowly and deeply. As you do this, ask the cards to provide you with help and insight during your reading, and focus on everything you want to ask. If you are reading for someone else, ask them to think of their question, and focus on their energy. If you or the person you are reading for don't have a specific question, simply ask the cards for any helpful guidance or reassurance they can provide.

Do this for a few moments, and then spread the cards face down in a fan shape, selecting those you feel most drawn to until you have the number needed for your chosen spread. You can either do this with your eyes open, or by closing your eyes and gently moving your hands over the deck, then seeing which card(s) your hand naturally gravitates toward. If you are reading for someone else, spread the cards and ask them to pick the ones they feel drawn to. Alternatively, you can cut the deck into three piles, and choose the one you feel most guided to. Gather the other two piles together and place your chosen pile on top; then, when selecting the cards, draw from the top of the deck.

Place the remainder of the deck to one side, and turn the chosen cards over one at a time. Trust your gut reactions to each card, and pay attention to any names, places, phrases, or images that pop into your mind.

Once you've finished the reading, thank your cards for their insights and guidance, and give the deck a final shuffle to clear its energy. Extinguish any candles or incense you've used, and place the cards in a safe box or drawer until you want to use them again.

FINISHING A READING

This light meditation will help you close yourself down psychically after a reading. It can take as much or as little time as you like, and is also a great technique for helping you relax and switch off at the end of the day.

Begin by sitting comfortably in a quiet room while holding your cards, and lighting a candle to help you relax. Close your eyes, and start breathing deeply. Do this for a few moments until you feel completely calm and serene.

When you're ready, start to visualize a white light glowing around you, and gently going through your body and warming each part individually. Focus on each area separately, and feel a wave of relaxation going through your body.

Take a few more deep breaths, and then imagine a beautiful green light appearing around your heart. Visualize it becoming clearer in your mind, and focus all your energy on its color. Affirm: "I thank my cards for their guidance and wisdom."

Once you've done this, picture the green light slowly becoming smaller until it completely disappears. Take a deep breath, and visualize yourself being placed in a bubble of protective energy until you next connect.

THE SPREADS

The following spreads will help you get started on your Tarot journey. If you're new to Tarot, try starting with some of the simpler spreads, like the one-card reading below, and then move on to the longer ones when you're feeling more confident. Alternatively, choose the one you feel most drawn to, or you feel will be most helpful for you or the querent.

ONE-CARD READING

This classic one-card spread is ideal for times when you need a quick answer to a question, or would simply like some guidance for the day ahead. You can also use this technique to pick an inspiring affirmation to focus on each day.

Find a quiet space, and take a few deep breaths until you feel calm, centered, and relaxed. Shuffle the cards and ask for any guidance or insight they can provide for the day ahead. Alternatively, if there's a specific question you'd like to ask, repeat it several times in your mind.

Now select your card using your preferred technique (see page 5). Once you've chosen your card, turn it over, and look up its interpretation. Make a note of the card and its interpretation in a journal, and also jot down anything else that pops into your mind. Even if it doesn't make sense to you now, it may later on, so it's always worth writing down.

PAST, PRESENT, FUTURE

This time-honored three-card layout is a wonderful way of exploring you—or the querent's—past, present, and future. You can either focus on a particular issue or ask the cards for a general insight into the influences affecting you and your life at the time.

The first card, symbolizing the past, will highlight any past events that have led to your current situation, or are still impacting you now, while the second card, representing the present, will focus on the issues influencing your life today—and how to navigate your way through them. The third card, indicating the future, will suggest the likeliest outcome based on how things are now. But remember, this is by no means set in stone, and can change depending on your freewill and actions, so don't be too disheartened if the outcome isn't what you were hoping for.

Begin by shuffling the deck, and asking for insight into your past, present, and future. Select three cards using your preferred technique (see page 5), and lay them out as shown below. Turn them over one at a time, and interpret their meanings based on their positions in the spread.

1 Past   2 Present   3 Future

The Spreads 7

THE NORDIC COMPASS

The Nordic Compass spread is perfect for times when you're looking for a quick insight into your love and work lives. Start with the four cards suggested below, and if there's an area you'd like more insight into, such as work or love, add a second card for that position.

Begin by shuffling your cards, and asking for clarity about a specific situation or simply for some guidance about your life at present. Select your cards using your preferred technique (see page 5), and lay them out as shown below. Turn the cards over one by one, and begin your interpretation using the guide below.

1 North: Present-day situation

3 West: Relationships

2 South: Work and money

4 East: Outcome

8 The Spreads

THE HORSESHOE

This horseshoe-shaped spread will offer you guidance on the key areas in your life, from your relationships and work to your home life and friendships. If there's an aspect of your life you'd like further insight into, add a second card for that position.

Start by shuffling your cards, and asking for guidance about your relationships and work/home life. Select your cards using your preferred technique (see page 5) and lay them out as shown below. Turn them face up, and begin your interpretation using the guide below.

2 Relationships

1 Personal affairs

6 Outcome

3 Business/work/career

4 Home life

5 People around you

The Spreads 9

THE LIGHT WITHIN

This insightful layout will shine light on any areas in your life you may need to focus on, and is a great spread to turn to when you're seeking some clarity or guidance. Take note of the cards you select, and think about what each one is guiding you to do.

Spend a few moments breathing deeply, and focus on calming your mind. Shuffle the cards, and ask for any guidance they can offer for your higher good. Select your cards using your preferred technique (see page 5) and lay them out as shown on the right. Turn them over one by one, and interpret their meanings using the guide on the right.

1 Clarity

2 Insight

3 Communication

4 Emotions

5 Intuition

6 Creativity

7 Structure

THE CLOCK

This clock-shaped spread will give you a deep insight into your life at present, and offer you help and guidance with any obstacles or challenges that may be holding you back.

Sit comfortably and shuffle your cards, while thinking of your question, or asking for any guidance they can offer. Select your cards using your preferred technique (see page 5), and lay them out as shown below. Once you've done this, repeat the process twice, so you have three cards in each position.

Three is the number of change, so the cards selected will highlight any developments in your life, and empower you to make any changes necessary.

Focus on each position at a time, and turn all three cards over (beginning with the one you feel most drawn to), before moving on to the next position. When reading the cards for each position, try to link them together and create a story. Take your time to focus on each position individually, and interpret the cards' meanings using the guide below.

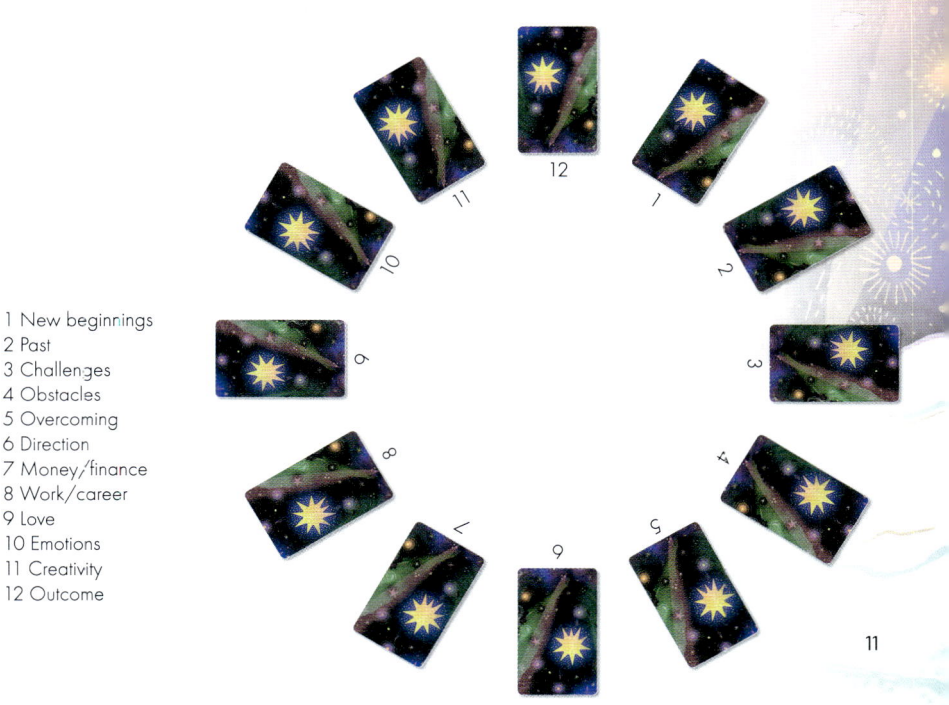

1 New beginnings
2 Past
3 Challenges
4 Obstacles
5 Overcoming
6 Direction
7 Money/finance
8 Work/career
9 Love
10 Emotions
11 Creativity
12 Outcome

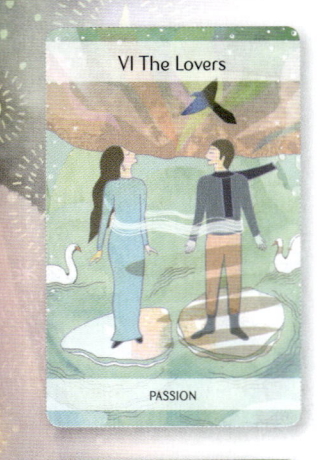

THE MAJOR ARCANA

The Major Arcana cards represent a journey through life, and will guide and empower you through your own, marking key events and turning points. The journey starts with an exciting adventure (symbolized by the Fool), and passes through periods of uncertainty and introspection (signified by cards such as the Moon and the Hermit), times when your faith may be tested (shown by the Tower and Death), and times of happiness and joy (denoted by the Sun and the World).

There are traditionally 78 cards in a Tarot deck—22 Major Arcana and 56 Minor Arcana (see page 36). However, this deck features an additional card in the Major Arcana, Charity (see page 35). Charity is about kindness and generosity—to others and also to yourself—a theme which is not necessarily prominent in the traditional Major Arcana and which I felt should be included as it is an important concept for us all.

In this deck, the Nordic imagery is complemented by symbolic animals, from wolves (for protection) to owls (for wisdom), which provide a deeper insight into the cards' meanings. A keyword is included on each card, indicating its main theme at a glance.

The interpretations on pages 13–35 are accompanied by an inspiring message for each card and other keywords, which will guide and enrich your readings. You will also be given an insight into the rich and magical history of Nordic mythology, including legends about the Northern Lights and stories about the Nordic gods and goddesses, through the facts provided alongside each card's meaning.

If you're a beginner, you may wish to start by only using the Major Arcana in your spreads until you are familiar with them and feel ready to move on to the other cards.

0 The Fool

The Fool stands in an ice field, gazing at the Northern Lights. Enchanted, he watches as the bright lights gently move toward the ice, reflecting the ancient Nordic belief that the world began its journey (as the Fool is doing now) as fire and ice, before the two collided and created the world and its first inhabitant. A white wolf, symbolizing protection, accompanies him. Dressed in simple clothes, he is open to anything (and everything), and bravely steps out into the world full of excitement and hope.

KEYWORDS Innocence, journey, enthusiasm, optimism, joyfulness

MESSAGE "My journey through life starts now."

MEANING The Fool represents the start of a new journey—in work, love, or even location. A leap of faith will be required, as you turn away from what's comfortable and embrace the unknown. New relationships, exciting job offers, and opportunities to live and work in exotic places can all be expected, and this is a great omen for anyone who is thinking of starting a business or changing their career path. Encouraging you to be daring and brave, yet practical, it symbolizes the start of a new and exciting chapter in your life.

NEW BEGINNINGS

According to Nordic myths, the first inhabitant of the world was a god-like giant called Ymir, who gave birth to the other gods after drinking some milk and sleeping.

I The Magician

The Magician juggles two balls of free-flowing energy. Empowered, excited, and full of enthusiasm, he is ready to become the master of his own destiny. A large Nordic compass sits on the floor before him, with images of various rune stones, representing opportunities, adorning the outer rim. The points of the compass represent the different directions he can take, while the images of the four Tarot suits symbolize all he needs to manifest his hopes and dreams.

KEYWORDS Juggling, pros and cons, manifesting, talkative, charming

MESSAGE "I'm juggling my fate."

MEANING You have all the ingredients you need for success; now is the time to put them together, and create something spectacular! Perfectly timed messages, strokes of good luck, and chance encounters with the right people at the right time can all be expected, as the universe brings amazing opportunities—for love, work, and business—right to your door. Those in relationships can also expect lots of exciting surprises, including romantic trips abroad and thoughtful gestures, while a friend's clever matchmaking could lead to love for singletons.

Known as the "Vegvisir," the Nordic compass is thought to have originated from Iceland in the 17th century, and was often used to provide spiritual guidance.

II The High Priestess

The High Priestess sits at a table with precious stones and a crystal ball before her. Her hair is crimson red, eyes bright blue, and she is wearing a black cloak adorned with teal feathers. An eagle, representing her spiritual power, sits on her shoulder, while two cats (one black, one white)—her familiars—sit on either side of her. There is a full moon and sky full of stars in the distance, and a sword lies on the ground beside her. With the soul of a goddess and mind of a warrior, she symbolizes the balance between our inner and outer power.

KEYWORDS Spirituality, intuition, meditation, higher-self, healing

MESSAGE "I am guided by my intuition."

MEANING The High Priestess is the keeper of secrets! Listen to your intuition now, as all that glistens around you may not be gold. Secret information will soon be revealed, and what's hidden will be exposed. Privacy and discretion will be of utmost importance, as secrets will be shared, and loyalties may be tested. Messages from the universe are also likely, so take note of any recurring dreams or quotes you see as they could be signs. Your psychic powers will also be heightened; this card can predict a future career in healing or mediumship, too.

The Nordic gods and goddesses would often wear clothing made from feathers or fur, believing it would help them take on the characteristics of the animals.

III The Empress

III The Empress

NURTURE

In Nordic folklore, it was said that seeing the Northern Lights could ease the pain of childbirth.

The Empress sits in a meadow filled with pretty flowers. Three rabbits, synonymous with fertility, happily surround her. Dressed in a beautiful feminine gown, she gently cradles her stomach and smiles gratefully. The Northern Lights sparkle above her, while the mountains, representing difficulties, appear small and distant in the background. Happy and full of excitement, she represents the "birth" of a new and abundant phase in your life.

KEYWORDS Fertility, family, earth mother, love, creativity

MESSAGE "I am loved and happy."

MEANING The Empress can symbolize the "birth" of anything—from a new romance or business, to a new job or actual baby. New relationships and friendships can both be expected, while your desire to create—through writing, drawing, painting, or music—could also be heightened. Finances and businesses will also blossom, and there could be a chance to move to a larger property. That said, this card can also represent a literal pregnancy, so if you're hoping to start a family, now is the time. If not, be careful!

IV The Emperor

The Emperor is the "father figure" of the deck; strong, powerful, and fiercely protective of those he loves, he sits on a majestic ice throne, gazing proudly over his kingdom. A large Nordic compass, symbolizing his knowledge, lies on the ground beneath him, while a beautiful snowy owl, synonymous with protection, sits silently on a branch in the background. Always a leader and never a follower, he holds a crystal sphere in his left hand and a magic wand, representing his confidence, in his right; he seeks no-one's counsel but his own.

KEYWORDS Knowledge, guidance, wisdom, clarity, leadership

MESSAGE "Knowledge is the key to success."

MEANING The Emperor symbolizes stability and a return to order. Prepare to step into a leadership role, as opportunities to take the driving seat—in work and home life—head your way. Promotions, business awards, and milestone achievements in your work/studies are all likely, while those in relationships can expect a long-term commitment from their partners as well. Disputes with others will also be settled, and love could blossom with an older person for singletons, too. Listen to your head rather than heart now, as logic must outweigh emotion.

The Nordic god of poetry and war, Odin, was sometimes referred to as the "All-father." He is often depicted with a magical spear, known as the Gungnir.

The Major Arcana 17

V The Hierophant

The Hierophant stands between two pillars, as a couple, seeking his blessing, graciously bow down before him. A healer of hearts and teacher of life, he thrives on sharing his wisdom with others, and seeks to unify, rather than divide, those around him. An eagle, symbolizing his spiritual connection, flies high in the background, while a soft glow, representing his healing powers, emanates from his heart. The couple, hopeful and excited, sit quietly before him, as his blessings flow through them and unify their hearts.

KEYWORDS Learning, spiritual connection, union, healing, togetherness

MESSAGE "I am guided by knowledge."

MEANING The Hierophant symbolizes a period of personal development. Opportunities to expand your mind will be everywhere—from emails about new courses, to eye-opening articles and conversations with others. Your desire to learn through researching or studying will be higher than ever, and you may feel drawn to enhancing your spiritual gifts, too. Exciting developments in love, including marriage, are also possible, while those who are single could meet someone through a course or spiritual community. This card can also represent the need to conform.

Thor was the god of thunder; his legendary hammer had the power to heal as well as harm, and he often used it to bless weddings.

VI The Lovers

Two lovers stand on jagged pieces of ice in a deserted lake. Distracted and emotionally elsewhere, the woman appears to be turning away, while the man, bewitched by his partner, only has eyes for her. Physically together, but emotionally apart, they're joined together by a thread, which symbolizes their bond, but separated by the water, which represents their emotions. Two swans, signifying hope, are swimming nearby, while a bird of prey, sensing trouble in paradise, lurks dangerously overhead.

KEYWORDS Soulmates, choices, love, freedom, emotions

MESSAGE "I am entwined with passion."

MEANING The Lovers is a card of emotions, choices—and emotional choices! It marks a time when an important decision will need to be made in your love, work, or home life. Dilemmas about jobs and relationships are both possible, as tempting new offers rock the boat, and create a tsunami of emotions. Stable relationships will become stronger, while those in unhappy ones may part ways. Declarations of love from ex-partners and secret admirers are also likely, while those looking for romance could meet their dream mate at a wedding or engagement party.

The goddess of spring and eternal youth, Idun, was thought to have magical apples that would help the gods and goddesses stay young and beautiful forever.

VII The Chariot

A young woman stands upon a chariot. Confident, courageous, and full of ambition, she knows what she wants, and nothing (and no one) can stop her. Two dogs—her spiritual guardians and faithful companions—stand in front of the chariot, awaiting their mistress's instructions. Her heart and mind, symbolized by the images of the sun and moon, are in perfect alignment. She is finally on the right path, and prepared for both the light and dark parts of the journey ahead.

KEYWORDS Journey, conflicted, indecision, choices, direction

MESSAGE "I decide my destiny."

MEANING You know what you want; now is the time to grab it with both hands, for your chariot awaits! Everything you need—courage, confidence, and determination—are already within you. There is no room for fear or doubt. A long journey lies ahead; either toward something you desire or away from something you don't. Self-belief is essential right now. Master your emotions, and you will master your fate. Obstacles will be overcome with inner (rather than outer) strength, and the potential for victory is great.

The Nordic goddess of the sun (Sol) and god of the moon (Mani) were siblings who would pull the sun and moon across the sky in chariots.

20 The Major Arcana

VIII Justice

A woman wearing a red cloak stands in the middle of a snowy landscape. Her expression, like the snow around her, is as cold as ice, and she is holding a scale, symbolizing justice. Neither a hero nor villain, she is simply karma personified. A black bear, signifying strength and inner wisdom, stands beside her. Like the bear—which can either protect and guard its companion, or savagely hurt and attack them—this card symbolizes the way our choices and actions determine the outcome of the scales.

KEYWORDS Strength, fairness, legal issues, pros and cons, decisions

MESSAGE "I am fair and honest."

MEANING Synonymous with truth, this card symbolizes justice prevailing—and karma being served. The truth of a matter, whether it's in your favor or not, will soon be revealed, and someone will be held accountable. If you have been wronged, you will get justice. If you have wronged another, they will get theirs. Either way, the situation will be resolved, and the fairest outcome can be assured. Someone's true colors could also be revealed, and a difficult decision may need to be made. This card can also signify the need for more balance in your life.

Nordic warriors would often wear clothing made from wild bears' skin to help them become indestructible in battles.

IX The Hermit

The Hermit sits under a beautiful waterfall. Undisturbed and completely content in his own company, he sits in quiet meditation, peacefully channeling his inner guidance and wisdom. A hare, symbolizing intuitive messages and spiritual knowledge, sits beside him, while a roe deer, signifying spiritual growth and divine guidance, can be seen in the background. Completely isolated from the world around him, he cherishes "being" over doing, and spiritual abundance over material riches.

KEYWORDS Isolation, meditation, withdrawal, contemplation, reflection

MESSAGE "Take time to breathe and contemplate your next move."

MEANING Known as a card of soul-searching, the Hermit marks a time when you need to switch off your phone, log off social media, and enjoy some much-needed alone time. Spiritual practices, like journaling and meditating, may call to you now, and your appetite for learning and writing will be insatiable. Time spent in nature will also replenish your energy, while a mentor could offer you some invaluable guidance, too. Think twice before making any decisions and be patient; the answers will come when you're ready.

The Nordic Tree of Life was thought to have three wells under it, all of which would water its roots and keep it alive.

X The Wheel of Fortune

The Wheel of Fortune depicts three women sitting around a well and weaving in unison. Inspired by an ancient Nordic myth, the card pays homage to the legend of three ladies (known as the Norns) who would determine people's fates by weaving them into a tapestry. Each thread was thought to represent a human life. The Tree of Life, symbolizing growth, stands tall behind them, while butterflies, synonymous with transformation, can be seen flying around in the background, carrying messages of hope in their wings.

KEYWORDS Destiny, divine intervention, luck, changes, progress

MESSAGE "Trust in fate."

MEANING The Universe is on your side right now—and anything is possible! Lucky windfalls and serendipitous encounters can both be expected, as the weavers of fate stitch an abundance of blessings into your destiny. Promotions and pay rises are equally possible, while those looking for work could get an exciting job offer, too. Businesses will thrive, while a chance encounter could lead to love for singletons. Your intuition will also be heightened, and this card can predict a new home or relocation overseas as well.

FATE

According to the myth, the names of the three women were Urd, Verdandi, and Skuld, roughly translating to past, present, and future in old Norse.

XI Strength

According to the myth, Fenrir's magical ribbon was created from a combination of six "impossible" ingredients, including the breath of a fish and beard of a woman!

A woman gazes into the eyes of a wolf and holds his mouth open, while he sits beside her calmly, with a ribbon tied around him. The image is based on the legend of a wolf called Fenrir, who was so strong that he couldn't be restrained. The Gods eventually found a chain strong enough to bind him, which looked like a ribbon but was stronger than iron. While the story itself had a grizzly ending (let's just say a hand was lost!), it serves as a beautiful reminder that strength can't always be seen, and is often found within.

KEYWORDS Power, strength, ego, precision, courage

MESSAGE "Believe in yourself."

MEANING The Strength card denotes a time when you may need to protect the people you love, including yourself, from the negative forces around them. Your patience will be tested as other people's actions push you to the limit. Old insecurities could also resurface, and follow you around, like bullies in a playground. Gentle coercion rather than force is essential now, both with yourself and others. Aggression will only add fuel to the fire; compassion will calm it. So be patient; their actions will determine their karma; yours will determine your own.

XII The Hanged Man

A man hangs upside down from the Tree of Life. Beneath the tree's roots lies a well, thought to contain all the knowledge of the universe. Four deer, symbolizing spiritual growth and innocence, can be seen nibbling on the tree's leaves, while an eagle, synonymous with wisdom and high aspirations, sits upon one of the branches. Like the Nordic God Odin—who sacrificed nine days and nights, as well as his eye, for spiritual wisdom from the same well—the Hanged Man is willing to do whatever it takes to gain the knowledge he seeks.

KEYWORDS Static, comfortable, surrender, contentment, trust

MESSAGE "I am too comfortable."

MEANING: The Hanged Man is a card of patience, surrender, and, most importantly, faith. The Universe could seem like it has left and gone on vacation now, as life slows down and a situation in love, work, or business reaches a standstill. Frustrating delays are likely, as decisions from others take longer than expected, and you could feel like you're stuck in limbo. Pause and view the situation differently. You may not be able to control what happens, but you can control your experience of it. So, accept the now—and have faith in what's to come.

According to Nordic tales, there was a naughty squirrel (Ratatoskr) that would travel up and down the Tree of Life, stirring up trouble between the eagle at the top and the serpent at the bottom!

XIII Death

In Nordic mythology, Hell was a cold and icy place, rather than a place filled with flames and fire.

A woman stands on top of a jagged ice block. Dressed in black, she stares ahead without emotion, as wild flames burn around her. Trapped spirits are locked inside the block beneath her, while sharks, synonymous with fear, lurk dangerously nearby. The ocean, once so peaceful and calm, is now on fire, and the sky has become red and unsettled. However, like the Goddess of the Underworld, Hel, whose name means "one that hides," the Death card suggests there could be a hidden lesson or blessing in the chaos.

KEYWORDS Transformation, release, endings, change, new beginnings

MESSAGE "Every ending has a new beginning."

MEANING The Death card signifies the end of one era and birth of another. A season of change can be expected, as a divine intervention removes a situation that no longer serves you (such as a toxic job or relationship) to create space for something that will. Whatever is meant to stay, will stay; whatever isn't, won't. The ending is likely to be abrupt and beyond your control—such as a sudden break up, or unavoidable house move. Do not fight the changes; the more you do, the harder it will be. In time you'll see they were a blessing in disguise.

XIV Temperance

A young woman stands before a lake, and cautiously tests the water. With one foot in and one foot out, symbolizing her emotional needs and earthly demands, she's ready to let go of the old and welcome the new. A large house, representing her old beliefs and foundations, stands tall behind her, while a small salmon, synonymous with healing, swims happily in the water. Beautiful flowers, signifying her growth, can be seen dancing in the background, while her spirit animal, a horse (known for its strength) watches her from a distance.

KEYWORDS Healing, emotions, balance, serenity, patience

MESSAGE "I heal others by healing myself."

MEANING Temperance is a card of balance. It often appears when the pressures of life become too heavy to carry, and the actions of others start disrupting your peace. Whether it's cancelling plans in order to stay home, or simply taking a few days off to relax, it marks a time when healthy boundaries are key, and your well-being needs to come first. Unreasonable demands from others are likely, and there could be some discord around you, too. Breathe and keep calm; for this too shall pass, and your outer world will match your inner one once again.

XIV Temperance

HARMONY

The spirit animals of the Nordic god Odin were two ravens called Huginn and Muninn, meaning "thought" and "memory."

XV The Devil

XV The Devil

BOUNDARIES

The god of thunder, Thor, was renowned for his hot temper. In fact, his rages were so powerful they were thought to create lightning and thunder!

A man is surrounded by spikes of ice, as a whirlwind of forceful energy wraps itself around him. Blinded by his fear, he fails to see the opening to the side of him, and desperately clings on to a rope of spiraling energy, which merely pulls him even deeper into the vortex. A white owl, synonymous with wisdom, sits in a cage beside him. Like her companion, she longs to escape, but is so lost in her distress, she doesn't realize that its door is open. Both trapped and both able to escape, the Devil and the owl symbolize the emotional prisons we create in our minds.

KEYWORDS Addiction, lust, passion, self-harm, restriction

MESSAGE "Find your own truth."

MEANING The Devil is a card of entrapment. It symbolizes a time when you are feeling trapped or disempowered by a situation or relationship; what was once a dream may now seem like a nightmare, which is no longer worth fighting for or trying to repair. It can represent anything from a toxic relationship or job, to an unhealthy friendship or affair. However, while the situation may no longer be salvageable, your happiness definitely is. So be brave, and walk away from anything that binds you—in mind, body, or spirit.

XVI The Tower

A beautiful castle stands in an ice field. Once strong, sturdy, and powerful, it is now burning to ashes on one side. A dragon, symbolizing destruction, can be seen laughing among the flames. The other side remains firm and strong—affected by the attack, but not destroyed by it. Like the Nordic warriors, whose legacies were often defined by fighting dragons (either making them heroes if they were victorious, or costing them their lives if they weren't), the Tower symbolizes the breaking and rebuilding of your character.

KEYWORDS Destruction, endings, fear, restriction, freedom

MESSAGE "My foundations are strong."

MEANING A card of fate and forces beyond our control, the Tower symbolizes a dramatic and unforeseen turn of events. Change and upheaval are likely now, as the fragile foundation of a situation—in love, work, or finance—inevitably collapses. This card can indicate the loss of a job, end of a relationship, or closure of a business. However, like the Nordic gods, who believed the world would end during a final battle before a new one would emerge, it signifies that you, too, can (and will) rise from these difficulties—happier, wiser, and stronger than ever.

FOUNDATION

It was believed an evil dragon-like serpent (named Nidhogg) lurked at the bottom of the Tree of Life, savagely feasting on its roots.

XVII The Star

According to old Finnish myths, the Northern Lights were created by a little Firefox, who ran so quickly across the snow that his tail caused sparks!

A young woman stands in a deserted ice field, and looks up at the Northern Lights. Mesmerized by the bright colors, she reaches her hand toward the star-lit sky. Her spirit animal, a majestic stag—synonymous with strength—watches over her from afar. Protected by her guides and empowered by her faith, she is exactly where she's meant to be. The stars, symbolizing her wishes and dreams, glisten brightly above her.

KEYWORDS Dreams, fulfillment, hope, healing, beauty

MESSAGE "My wishes and dreams have come true."

MEANING The Star brings calm after chaos and light after darkness. Synonymous with hope and healing, it often appears following a period of sadness, and marks the start of a brighter time in your life. Miracles will appear wherever they're needed, from amazing new job offers to reconciliations with ex-partners. Finances will also flourish, while any rocky patches between partners will be done and dusted. Those in creative fields, such as art or music, will be given their chance to shine, and this card can also predict a future career in healing.

XVIII The Moon

The Moon shines brightly in the sky, as the stars sparkle around it. Silhouettes of dancing figures, which represent the souls of young maidens, soldiers, and children, can be seen laughing and waving among the bright colors and twinkling lights. Two red foxes, excited by the pretty colors, can be seen gazing longingly at the sky, while a king crab, symbolizing mystery, secrecy, hidden worlds, and the subconscious, warily climbs onto a rock below.

KEYWORDS Subconscious, reflection, self-defeat, sadness, depression

MESSAGE "I reflect negative emotions."

MEANING Like the moon, which is always part hidden, this card encourages you to trust your instincts, as everything may not be as it seems. Hidden truths about a situation or person will soon be revealed, and your heart may need to accept something your mind already knows. Negative thoughts could run wild in your mind, and buried emotions, such as childhood insecurities, may resurface. Take a step back and let things unfold naturally. The truth will soon be revealed, and you will know fact from fiction.

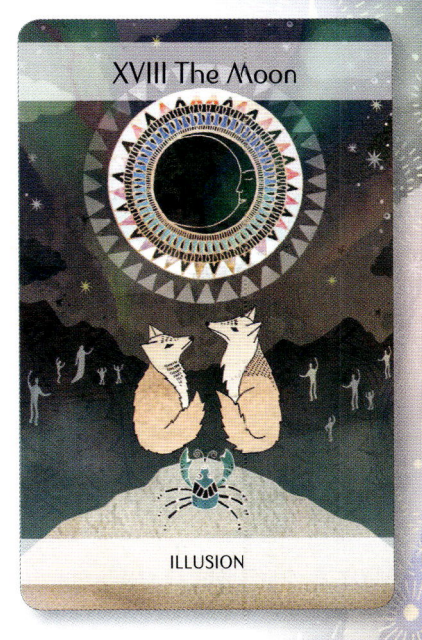

XVIII The Moon

ILLUSION

Many people believed the Northern Lights were the souls of brave soldiers who had died in battle.

XIX The Sun

The goddess of fertility, Frigg, is thought to have been so heartbroken when her beloved son Baldur was killed by a dart made from mistletoe that her tears turned into white berries, forming the plant as we know it now.

A boy and girl sit together happily building a snow castle, while the sun, synonymous with happiness, shines brightly in the sky. Innocent and filled with childlike wonder, the children are completely content in their own little paradise. Squirrels, representing fun and playfulness, can be seen dancing around in the background, while beautiful flowers, symbolizing joyful times, sway around them in harmony. Dressed in cozy garments, signifying the warmth of their loved ones, the children are surrounded by love and happiness.

KEYWORDS Light, happiness, joy, family, love

MESSAGE "I am happy and successful."

MEANING The Sun is a card of family and happy occasions. It marks a joyful period in your life when you can pop open the bubbly and celebrate with friends and loved ones. Pregnancies and births are both possible, and it can predict a vacation abroad or time spent with children, too. Reunions with childhood friends and long-lost relatives are also likely, and an estranged couple could rekindle their love as well. A vacation or wedding overseas may lead to love for singletons, while a proposal might be on the way for couples.

XX Judgment

A young woman studies her reflection in a lake, while a caterpillar, synonymous with rebirth, sits on a leaf nearby. Calm and full of compassion for her younger self, she is ready to let go of her regrets, and make peace with her past. Her reflection, symbolizing how she perceives herself now, smiles up at her from the water below—stronger, wiser, and kinder to herself than before. The lake, representing her past, lies peacefully before her, while the trees, signifying her growth, stand tall and strong at the edge of the water.

KEYWORDS Second chances, guilt, reflection, betrayal, insecurity

MESSAGE "I forgive myself and others."

MEANING The Judgment card denotes a time of healing, second chances, and rebirth. Mixed emotions can be expected, as old doors reopen, and faces from the past return. Trusting your own judgment will be of utmost importance now, as big decisions will need to be made. Blasts from the past are likely, including messages from exes, and dreams about old school friends. Pause, reflect, and look back before you move forward. You'll soon know which chapters to revisit, and which ones to close once and for all.

The Valkyrie, a powerful tribe of women, decided the fate of fallen warriors, and judged whether they were worthy of joining Odin's army in the final battle between the gods. Some said the Northern Lights were reflections of their armor.

XXI The World

There were nine worlds in Nordic mythology, all of which were linked together by the Tree of Life, Yggdrasil.

The full moon, representing the World, shines brightly in the sky, while the Northern Lights—unable to contain their excitement—dance happily around it. Silhouettes of animals, from foxes and hares, to horses, stags, and wolves, can be seen playing across its surface, while glimpses of laughing figures, symbolizing the souls of departed loved ones, cheerfully wave and celebrate from the sparkly lights. Filled with joy and happiness, the World dances in bliss and rejoices, as one cycle ends, and a new one begins.

KEYWORDS Journey, movement, change, endurance, completion

MESSAGE "The world is your oyster."

MEANING You've achieved your heart's desire—now's the time to bask in your glory, and enjoy your success! Synonymous with happiness and fulfillment, the World can indicate anything from an engagement or birth, to a milestone birthday, anniversary, or career achievement. Promotions, business awards, and recognition from high places can be expected, and it can predict a new home, or relocation abroad, too. Proposals are also possible, while love could blossom with a foreign stranger for singletons.

XXII Charity

Designed by the world-renowned artist Tracey Emin (see page 4), the Charity card depicts the image of one of the most sacred animals in Nordic mythology, a blue cat. Synonymous with the goddess of love and beauty, Freya, who's thought to have traveled in a chariot pulled by cats, felines were highly prized by ancient Nordic people, who believed the cats had been given to Freya as a gift from Thor. She loved them so much that they soon became her favorite companions, leading to them becoming a Nordic symbol of giving and kindness.

KEYWORDS Giving, kindness, compassion, independence

MESSAGE "What you give, you will receive."

MEANING Charity is a card of compassion and self-care. Like a cat, well known for its independence, this card encourages you to rely on yourself, rather than others, for the love and nurturing you seek. Acts of kindness, both to yourself and others, are essential now. Gifts and thoughtful gestures from others are equally likely. Your intuition may be heightened, and your desire to paint or write may be strengthened, too; days spent alone will recharge your energy. This card can also signify the need to spend time with animals.

XXII Charity

GENEROSITY

The goddess Freya is thought to have had a magical necklace (known as the Brisingamen) that made her irresistible to men!

The Major Arcana 35

THE MINOR ARCANA

While the Major Arcana cards tend to reflect significant changes or turning points in your life, the Minor Arcana cards often symbolize daily events and particular people. To read the Minor Arcana cards, use their suits and numbers as described below, along with their colors, keywords, and meanings on pages 37-64, and your intuition to guide you. Write down any recurring themes you notice in a notebook or journal to create your own interpretations.

THE FOUR SUITS

There are four suits in the Minor Arcana—Pentacles, Cups, Wands, and Swords—and each suit has 14 cards (ten numbered cards and a King, Queen, Knight, and Page). Each suit is associated with a particular element, and reflects a different aspect of your life.

Suit	Element	Associations
Pentacles	Earth	Finances, work, home, and security
Cups	Water	Emotions, love, intuition, and relationships
Swords	Air	Mind, conflict, intellect, and decisions
Wands	Fire	Travel, action, growth, and creativity

THE NUMBERED CARDS

The numbered cards in the Minor Arcana tend to reflect specific situations, or influences affecting your life. Their numbers, along with their suits, can provide an insight into their meanings.

Ace: Beginnings and new opportunities
Two: Partnerships and dilemmas
Three: Recognition and teamwork
Four: Stability and rest
Five: Conflict and challenges
Six: Harmony and balance
Seven: Potential and patience
Eight: Progress and rewards
Nine: Heightened energy
Ten: Completion and endings

THE COURT CARDS

Known as the Court Cards, the Kings, Queens, Knights, and Pages often represent people in your life or individuals you will soon meet. However, they can also symbolize a general influence over your life at the time, or offer you guidance within an area of your life. For instance, the Queen of Swords is known for her inner strength and tough exterior, and can either represent someone around you who embodies those traits, or will appear when you need to be less emotional (like the Queen of Cups) and more assertive like her!

Ace of Pentacles

KEYWORDS Prosperity, ideas, growth, ambition

The Ace of Pentacles is a card of new beginnings, divine intervention, and luck. The gods of good fortune are blessing you right now, as wonderful opportunities to boost your finances come your way. Unexpected gifts, windfalls, and bonuses are all possible, and those looking for work could get their dream job, too. Profitable deals and prestigious clients can be expected for new and existing businesses; while any applications for loans, mortgages, or home purchases are likely to be signed, sealed, and approved. This card can also predict a new relationship, or an exciting phase in an existing one.

Two of Pentacles

KEYWORDS Choices, foundation, determination, business ideas

The Two of Pentacles often appears when there's a dilemma between two options, both of which have their own merits and pitfalls. It can signify a choice between two jobs, career paths, or places to live or study. Dilemmas about money, such as the cost of a home or budget for a wedding, are possible, and joint investments with partners, including mortgages, might need to be considered, too. Finances should be monitored regularly and thoroughly, as unexpected costs are likely, and you may need to budget your time and energy as carefully as your money to avoid feeling burnt out.

Three of Pentacles

KEYWORDS Achievements, study, focus, unity

The Three of Pentacles is a card of praise and recognition. The world is your stage right now—and this is your moment to shine! Whether you're about to launch a business, or just got your first book published, this is a time when your talents will finally be showcased to others, and the months of hard work (and endless coffees) will pay off. In a reading, this card can represent anything you've put your heart and soul into—from organizing an event or giving a speech to performing on stage, throwing a party, or remodeling your home. Take a bow and relish the applause; you deserve it all—and more.

Four of Pentacles

KEYWORDS Emotional wealth, happiness, foundation, comfort

The Four of Pentacles often appears following a period of financial hardship, and heralds the arrival of a happier time for you—and your bank balance! More certainty and less anxiety can be expected, as debts are paid, jobs are found, and temporary contracts are made permanent. Financial disputes over property, money, or land are likely to end favorably; while any cost-cutting measures, such as downsizing to a smaller home or forgoing vacations, could pay off. However, it can also signify the need to be less stingy with money, so prepare for the future, but remember to enjoy the present, too!

Five of Pentacles

KEYWORDS Defeat, money worries, fear, bad luck

Synonymous with poverty and isolation, the Five of Pentacles often signifies a period of financial hardship and stress. Unforeseen setbacks are likely, from cutbacks at work and business closures to unexpected legal bills and costly home repairs. Break-ups, betrayals, and family feuds are possible, and someone you love could turn their back on you. A card of inner turmoil and worry, it can also represent a fear of being abandoned, rejected, or shunned by the people you love. But do not lose hope; if the sun can rise after a storm, so can you.

Six of Pentacles

KEYWORDS Charity, goodwill, loyalty, money

The Six of Pentacles is a card of generosity, kindness, and goodwill. Acts of kindness from others—including money, gifts, and tokens of love and friendship—are likely, and someone from the past may help you with a present problem. Friends, bosses, and family members could offer you their time and guidance, and thoughtful gestures from strangers can be expected as well. A card of giving and receiving, it can also signify a time when you are helping those around you, whether it's by supporting a friend in need, donating to a charity, or volunteering for a worthy cause.

Seven of Pentacles

Keywords Determination, commitment, worry, compromise

The Seven of Pentacles symbolizes a crisis of faith before a milestone moment in your life. From wedding day jitters to doubting your ideas or the worthiness of a legal dispute or trial, it represents a time when the finish line is in sight, and you start questioning whether it will all be worth it. Spoiler alert; it will—so don't fall at the last hurdle! If you need to rest, rest; if you need to slow down, slow down. But do not give up, as success is just around the corner. It can also represent a fear of failure, and encourages you to believe in yourself—and your dreams.

Eight of Pentacles

KEYWORDS Movement, achievement, success, passion for business

The Eight of Pentacles is a card of accomplishment. It can symbolize anything from a landmark achievement in your work or studies, such as a promotion, degree, or gaining a new qualification, to a personal triumph, such as losing weight or running a marathon. Positive outcomes to exams and interviews can be expected, and there could be an opportunity to further your skills while boosting your bank balance, too! Known as a card of craftsmanship, it's also a great omen for those thinking of pursuing a different career path or turning a hobby—for example, baking or jewelry-making—into a business.

Nine of Pentacles

KEYWORDS Prosperity, generosity, acknowledgment, home life

A card of luxury, leisure, and material comfort, the Nine of Pentacles represents a time when you can finally relax, and enjoy the fruits of your labor. Whether it's by treating yourself to a new pair of shoes or a fancy watch, or simply by becoming a lady (or gentleman) who lunches, it signifies a period when all is well in your world, and you can finally indulge in some well-deserved "me" time. Financially independent and free from worry, you have nowhere to be, no one to please, and nothing to do. Enjoy! Known as the "happily ever after" card, it can also symbolize time spent decorating your home and precious moments with loved ones.

Ten of Pentacles

KEYWORDS Closeness, completion, love, self-awareness

The Ten of Pentacles is always a wonderful sight to behold and is thought to be one of the most positive cards in the deck. A card of luck, love, and happiness, it often represents two families coming together and becoming one. Weddings, pregnancies, and second marriages are all possible, and couples could decide to move in together, too. It can also represent generous gifts from family members and close friends, including the inheritance of a home or large sum of money. Additionally, Cupid could bring two people together at a wedding or party for a loved one.

The Minor Arcana 41

Page of Pentacles

KEYWORDS Listener, creative, passionate, organization

The Page of Pentacles is the bearer of positive news and opportunities to grow. With the fearlessness of a child and practicality of an adult, he is a student of life and master of reinvention. From pursuing a new career path to learning a new skill or furthering your education, he symbolizes the desire to learn, evolve, and experience more of the world. If there's someone you like, ask them out! If your relationship's lost its spark, spice things up! Positive news about finances, exams, or job interviews is likely, and a house could be bought or sold, too.

Knight of Pentacles

KEYWORDS Learning, prosperity, entrepreneur, manifestation

The Knight of Pentacles is a card of patience, commitment, and planning. The seeds for success have been planted; now's the time to water their roots and wait for them to blossom! Slow and steady progress, rather than instant results, should be expected—in love, work, and finance. Planning, budgeting, and forward thinking are essential, as investments made now may reap amazing rewards in the future. A promotion, dream home, or committed relationship could also be on the horizon, but might take longer than expected to materialize. Be patient—it'll be worth the wait.

Queen of Pentacles

KEYWORDS Wholeness, communication, knowledge, caring

The Queen of Pentacles is the nurturer of the deck. Kind, generous, and always there for the people she loves, she thrives on helping others, and is the eternally supportive friend we all need and hope for. She often represents a female friend, co-worker, or family member who will help you grow and prosper. Growth can be expected in all areas, from finance and business to love and family. New businesses will start to flourish, while those in relationships could receive some unexpected money, too. Synonymous with home and family, this card can also predict a marriage, pregnancy, or move to the countryside.

King of Pentacles

KEYWORDS Balance, honesty, advisor, wisdom

The King of Pentacles is the king of success; powerful, hard-working, and full of ambition, he is a fair and just leader who other people respect, rather than fear. Generous with money, but relentless in the pursuit of it, he often represents an older male—such as a boss, powerful business leader, or mentor—who will help and guide you on your path to success. Promotions, pay rises, and higher-paying work opportunities are all possible, and this a great omen for anyone who's hoping to buy their first home, too. It can also predict romance with a wealthy older woman/man, or greater security in an existing relationship.

Ace of Cups

KEYWORDS New love, beginnings, openness, love

The Ace of Cups is a card of love, relationships, and new beginnings. It can signify a birth, pregnancy, or falling in love. Engagements and weddings are both possible, while those looking for love could meet someone special at a christening or birthday party. Closer bonds with friends and loved ones can be expected, and someone you love could surprise you with a very grand gesture. Promotions and new job offers are also likely, and this card is a great omen for anyone who's thinking of starting a business, writing a book, or taking a leap of faith on a childhood dream, too.

Two of Cups

KEYWORDS Soulmate, fulfillment, love, balance

The Two of Cups symbolizes a powerful bond between two souls. A card of fate, synchronicity, and divine intervention, it often predicts (or confirms) the arrival of a soulmate or kindred spirit in your life. The Universe will be playing matchmaker right now—in love, work, and friendships. Deeper commitments in relationships, including proposals, can be expected, and a wonderful new relationship could be on the way for singletons, too. A card of unity rather than division, it can also signify the rekindling of an old relationship, and is a wonderful omen for business partnerships.

Three of Cups

KEYWORDS Celebration, fun, joy, happiness

The Three of Cups is a card of fun, celebration, and happy times. This is a time to let your hair down, forget your worries, and enjoy yourself with your friends and loved ones. If you're invited to a party, go; if you feel like flirting, flirt! A positive omen for love, it can also symbolize a milestone in your relationship, such as meeting each other's parents for the first time or attending your first wedding together as a couple. Romantic sparks could fly at a party, wedding, or social gathering for those looking for love, and this card can represent a reunion, promotion, or pregnancy, too.

Four of Cups

KEYWORDS Concentration, vision, motivation, mindfulness

The Four of Cups symbolizes an unfulfilled heart or mind; it appears when you're feeling disillusioned, discontent, or simply tired of life. Past heartbreaks might have tainted your perception of love, or your dream job/partner may have fallen short of the fairy tale you envisioned. Your doubts could be outweighing your faith, and the grass might seem greener everywhere else. Let go of the thoughts that make you feel powerless—feel the doubt, and do it anyway! Focus on the changes you can make, rather than begrudging the ones you can't. Opportunities are around you; open your eyes and see them.

Five of Cups

KEYWORDS Loss, depression, sadness, reflection

The Five of Cups is a card of loss. It often appears when you're mourning the end of a relationship or job or the loss of a loved one. Synonymous with regret, it represents a time when the past is holding you hostage, and negative thoughts are consuming your mind. The glass may seem half-empty—or it could feel like there's nothing in it at all. And yet, despite it all, you're still standing. Be brave; for while this card might symbolize heartache, it also holds promise for recovery from it. So cry, shout, and curse the world if you must, and then, when you're ready, dust yourself off and move on like the warrior you are.

Six of Cups

KEYWORDS Comfort, safety, family, friendship

The Six of Cups represents happy memories. It symbolizes a time when the past meets the present, and friendly ghosts from the past return. Childhood friends or long-lost family members could reenter your life, and unexpected messages from ex-partners are likely, too. Time spent with loved ones, reminiscing and sharing stories about the past, could leave you feeling nostalgic, and dreams about people and places you once loved might trigger old memories. This card can also signify a reconciliation with an old love, and is a great omen for those hoping to start a family.

Seven of Cups

KEYWORDS Inner guidance, disappointment, wishful thinking, confusion

This is a card of choices—or more specifically, too many of them! Romantically, it can predict several new love interests for singletons, while those in relationships could attract a new (and rather tempting) admirer. Otherwise, it can represent one or more job offers, or a dilemma about where to live. However, it can also symbolize wishful thinking, and often appears when you're romanticizing a situation. So take a step back and view things objectively; be brave and ask those difficult questions—even if they scare you. Once you do, for better or worse, you'll know where you stand.

Eight of Cups

KEYWORDS Opportunities, change, movement, motivation

The Eight of Cups signifies a time when you need to walk away from a situation that no longer fulfills you or brings you joy. A friendship, relationship, or family bond may have wilted long ago, or a job you once loved—or perhaps never did—could be leaving you feeling emotionally depleted. Your heart has already left; now it's time for your body to follow. Like a vase that's been broken, the situation is no longer what it once was, and trying to fix or rescue it will only hurt you further and delay the inevitable. You have done all you can to save the situation; now it's time to save yourself.

Nine of Cups

KEYWORDS Abundance, rewards, appreciation, accomplishment

The Nine of Cups is the Tarot's "wish card"; it can signify anything from finding your dream job, partner, or house to getting a promotion or winning an award. Anything is possible right now—in love, work, and home life. If there's something you want; now's the time to go for it! From joining a dating site to submitting a book proposal, this is a card where your hopes and wishes really do come true, and the gods and goddesses answer your prayers. Symbolizing a happy heart and grateful spirit, it can also predict joyful times with friends and loved ones, and a new relationship for singletons.

Ten of Cups

KEYWORDS Union, comfort, stability, uplifting

A card of happiness, harmony, and domestic bliss, the Ten of Cups symbolizes the fairy-tale ending—and happily ever after—of our favorite movies and childhood dreams. Synonymous with "happy families," it can predict an engagement, pregnancy, or new home for couples, and those looking for love could meet their Prince (or Princess) Charming. Happy occasions, such as weddings, christenings, and family reunions, could bring you and your loved ones closer together, while any animosity between you and those you love will soon be forgotten, too.

Page of Cups

KEYWORDS Joyfulness, child-like, kindness, friendship

The Page of Cups is the messenger. Fun, playful, and young at heart, he heralds the arrival of positive news. Exciting messages about pregnancies, engagements, and new romances can be expected—and you could hear some shocking gossip about someone you know, too! The Page of Cups can also predict romance with a younger person, and often appears when you've captured the heart of a secret admirer. Your creativity, intuition, and inspiration may be heightened, and the outcome to any interviews, tests, or exams is likely to be positive. New friendships can be expected.

Knight of Cups

KEYWORDS Idealistic, childish, imagination, creativity

The Knight of Cups is the hopeful romantic of the deck. Idealistic, charming, and charismatic, he follows his heart rather than head, and is the classic "knight in shining armor," bringing us hope of the happy ending we seek. A dreamer rather than thinker, he acts on emotion rather than reason, and often predicts the arrival of an exciting offer. Whirlwind romances, new work opportunities, and marriage proposals are all possible—and those looking for love could be swept off their feet by more than one suitor! But be cautious; people's words may not always translate into actions.

Queen of Cups

KEYWORDS Sensitivity, purity, family, serenity

The Queen of Cups is the queen of hearts; kind, caring, and full of compassion, she wears her heart on her sleeve, and is happiest when looking after those she loves. She usually represents a motherly figure in your life, such as an older friend, trusted co-worker, or female family member, who will always be there for you, no matter what. In a reading, she can predict a pregnancy, new relationship, or future career in healing, counseling, or nursing. Friends may also need your help and guidance; be there for those you love, but remember to be there for yourself, too.

King of Cups

KEYWORDS Emotion, love, loyalty, fairness

The King of Cups is the "voice of reason"; he is the wise, rational, and compassionate father-figure or trusted friend, who strikes the perfect balance between empathy and objectivity. His discernment, integrity, and good judgment are cherished by those around him, and he thrives on helping others while maintaining healthy boundaries. He often represents a teacher, spiritual advisor, or friend who will help and guide you. In a reading, he signifies the need to control your emotions. There could be some conflict around you. Stay calm. These storms will soon pass, and the sun will rise again.

Ace of Wands

KEYWORDS Creativity, spiritual wisdom, travel, energy

The Ace of Wands is a card of creativity, travel, and new beginnings. It can symbolize anything from the start of a new job or business, to the early stages of a creative project or new career path. Pregnancies and new relationships are likely, and it can predict a change in home. Exciting adventures abroad, including solo travels and activity-based trips, are possible, as well as an opportunity to live or work overseas. Those looking for love could meet their perfect match in a foreign land, too. Be brave, daring, and bold—and say yes to new adventures.

Two of Wands

KEYWORDS Communication, self-worth, partnership, confidence

The Two of Wands marks the start of a rewarding partnership in love, work, or business. From joint ventures with friends to new relationships and fruitful collaborations with others, it heralds a time when two heads are better than one, and joint projects are poised for success. Existing businesses will thrive as opportunities to grow and diversify come knocking, and an office romance could be on the cards for singletons as well. Important decisions will also need to be made, in work and romance, and there could be a choice between two partners or jobs. Don't settle for what's comfortable—choose happiness instead.

Three of Wands

KEYWORDS Travel, celebration, foundation, joy

The Three of Wands heralds the start of an exciting adventure. The sky's the limit right now—so spread your wings and fly! Proposals, weddings, and romantic encounters in exotic places are all possible, and this card can also predict an upcoming move to a new city or country. Businesses and work projects will flourish, while those in creative fields such as the arts, writing, or music, could get their "big break." New friendships and job offers can also be expected, and singletons could meet their Mr (or Ms) Right during a work trip abroad or vacation with a friend.

Four of Wands

KEYWORDS Invitations, new friends, exploration, trust

The Four of Wands predicts a time of love, laughter, and exciting celebrations with loved ones. The sweet scent of happiness will be in the air as invitations to birthdays, weddings, and anniversary parties head your way. Surprise parties and reunions with childhood friends are possible, and this card can also represent a relaxing break in a seaside village or small town. Housewarming parties and extended stays in family homes can be expected, and the outcome to any exams or interviews is likely to be positive. This card can also symbolize a honeymoon, new home, or community event.

Five of Wands

KEYWORDS Fights, frustration, stubbornness, ego

The Five of Wands is a card of rivalry, conflict, and strife. Disagreements with others can be expected as brewing tensions reach boiling point. Power struggles with others are likely—those in competitive fields such as journalism, fashion, or sports, could clash with their superiors, and rivalries in friendships and families are possible. This card can symbolize a love triangle for singletons. There could also be trouble in paradise for couples, as old insecurities and interfering third parties (including ex-partners) cause unnecessary arguments and tension. Stand your ground, but don't be pulled into other people's drama.

Six of Wands

KEYWORDS Confidence, accomplishment, creative vision, empowerment

The Six of Wands is one of the most positive cards in the deck. Known as the Tarot's "yes" card, it predicts victory in all areas. From winning a lawsuit to passing a driving test, it marks a triumphant moment in your life when you can celebrate and claim the crown that's rightfully yours. Promotions and high exam results are both possible, and it can even predict a moment of fame or TV appearance! Businesses will also be given their chance to shine as prestigious awards, celebrity endorsements, and media attention head their way, while those in creative fields may get their moment in the spotlight as well.

The Minor Arcana

Seven of Wands

KEYWORDS Self-belief, challenges, trust, calmness

The Seven of Wands is a card of opposition. It can represent anything from a friend or relative who dislikes your partner to a colleague who's constantly picking on you and causing trouble. Taking the high road will be of utmost importance as other people's childish antics and jealousy cause unnecessary drama in your life. Territorial behavior from others is likely, and difficulties with neighbors and in-laws are possible, too. Legal battles and bitter divorce settlements could cause tension, and this card can symbolize a high-pressured job, such as law, as well. Go where the love is, and leave the rest to karma.

Eight of Wands

KEYWORDS Movement, travel, self-awareness, opportunities

Known as a card of communication, the Eight of Wands marks the start of a busy period in your life. Prepare to be in high demand, as long-awaited messages, emails, and calls finally come your way. Favorable outcomes to job interviews and business proposals are both likely. Those looking for love could meet a promising new partner online or while traveling, and you may receive unexpected messages from ex-partners. Any delays to home moves or legal proceedings should be over soon. Pay attention to any messages you receive, as they could offer an opportunity in disguise.

Nine of Wands

KEYWORDS Resilience, inner strength, empowerment, challenges

The Nine of Wands is a card of perseverance and holding on. It represents a time when an ongoing battle has nearly been won, and you now need to defend what's yours. Small but frustrating setbacks are likely, as unexpected hurdles appear at the last minute. Opposition from others, including those you're working with, such as editors and designers, is possible, while those in relationships could be tested by an ex-partner's reappearance, too. Synonymous with perfectionism, this card can also symbolize a fear of being hurt or rejected by others. Protect yourself, but don't be afraid to let others protect you, too.

Ten of Wands

KEYWORDS Completion, vision, burdens, emotional freedom

The Ten of Wands symbolizes a time when you're feeling overwhelmed or burdened. It often appears when you're nearing the end of a mission or goal, and the final stages of your journey prove to be the most challenging of all. The cost of success could be greater than expected, as growth in one area, such as business or work, leads to neglect in others—perhaps friendships and love. Unreasonable demands from other people, including relatives and bosses, could leave you feeling exhausted, and there may be some unforeseen setbacks as well. Pause and reevaluate your priorities. Success is important, but so are the people you love.

Page of Wands

KEYWORDS Naïve, worrier, messages, playfulness

The Page of Wands heralds the arrival of positive messages. From flirty online exchanges to emails about new jobs and exciting courses, it marks a playful time in your life when you can just relax, have some fun, and act like a teenager again. Vacation romances, short-but-sweet flings, and harmless flirtations are all possible, and you could attract some flattering attention from a younger person, too! A childhood friend or teenage sweetheart might reenter your life, and singletons could be charmed by an artist, sports enthusiast, or musician. This card can also predict new friendships and a change in career path.

Knight of Wands

KEYWORDS Hot-headed, unwilling to change, spontaneity, immaturity

The Knight of Wands is the Tarot's wild child; daring, brave, and obsessed with his freedom, he lives life on the edge, and encourages you to do the same. Significant progress can be expected in all areas as life goes from zero to 100 quickly and dramatically! Exciting nights out, last-minute vacations, and fabulous parties are all on the horizon, while those looking for love could be swept off their feet by an exotic stranger. Job offers abroad, relocations overseas, and changes in residence are also possible. This is the perfect time to be brave like the Knight and try something daring, such as going on a blind date.

Queen of Wands

KEYWORDS Practical, nurturing, creative, polite

The Queen of Wands is the queen of passion! Full of energy and always on the go, she's the life and soul of every party, and brings fun and laughter wherever she goes. Confident, fiery, and fiercely loyal to the people she loves, she believes in herself wholeheartedly, and encourages you to do the same. She often represents an outgoing individual who will be your number one cheerleader in everything you do. One thing's for sure: you can certainly expect lots of excitement when she's around! Pregnancies and trips abroad are both likely, and your social life could be busier than ever, too.

King of Wands

KEYWORDS Dominant, determined, independent, honest

The King of Wands is the Tarot's rebel with a cause; passionate, well-traveled, and never afraid to stand out from the crowd, he fights for what he believes in, and isn't afraid of breaking the rules. A doer rather than thinker, he thrives on excitement and adventure, and is a natural born leader who doesn't bow down to anyone. He often represents a free-spirited individual who will motivate you to pursue your dreams. Whether it's asking someone on a date or quitting your job to become your own boss, this is a time to follow his example—and just go for it!

Ace of Swords

KEYWORDS Cutting through, structure, stability, victory

The Ace of Swords is the Tarot's "green light" card: if you've been waiting for a sign to do something, this is it! From writing a book to starting a business, now is the time to stop wishing and start doing. A card of acting, rather than dreaming, it empowers you to rely on yourself, rather than the universe or other people, to create the life you want. It can also signify the need to see people as they really are, rather than how you wish they would be. So be honest with yourself and others, and cut ties with anyone who poisons your spirit—or who never gives, but loves to receive.

Two of Swords

KEYWORDS Choices, pessimism, pathways, uncertainty

The Two of Swords is a card of difficult decisions. It symbolizes a time when you're torn between two options, and neither choice is ideal; you may need to choose between keeping the peace around you or finding peace within you. Ignoring the situation will only prolong the turmoil, so speak your truth, no matter how much it may hurt you or another. The sooner you rip off the Band-Aid, the sooner the healing can begin. A card of building (rather than burning) bridges, it can also signify the need to lay down your emotional armor, and allow yourself to love and be loved.

Three of Swords

KEYWORDS Heartache, tears, emotional pain, negative thoughts

The Three of Swords is a card of heartbreak. It signifies the loss of a relationship, job, or friendship. Your inner strength could be tested as a friend becomes a foe, lover becomes an enemy, or family member turns into a stranger. A hurtful truth might also be revealed, and the words or actions of others may cut deep, like a Nordic warrior's axe. Affairs and betrayals are possible, and the true colors of those you love will be revealed. However, like the Nordic Goddess Freya, who was set alight three times by those she helped and survived, it promises that you, too, will survive this.

Four of Swords

KEYWORDS Selfishness, healing, rest, peacefulness

A card of rest and recovery, the Four of Swords symbolizes the need to retreat and heal. If you're feeling burnt out, rest; if your job's stressing you out, take time off; if your partner's driving you crazy, spend time apart. This is a time to hit the pause button on your life, and take a much-needed break before the show must go on. A card of surrender, rather than control, it encourages you to refill your own cup before trying to fill anyone else's. So rest, recharge, and calm your body and mind; doing so may not change what tomorrow will bring, but it could change how you respond to it.

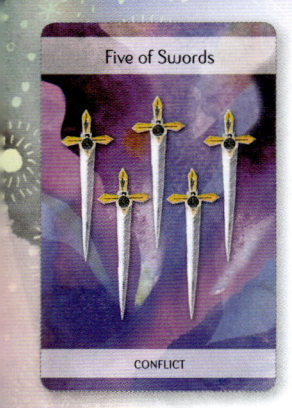

Five of Swords

KEYWORDS Anxiety, fear, worry, overwhelmed

The Five of Swords is a card of conflict, opposition, and defeat. It can represent anything from an ongoing family feud to a legal dispute or conflict with your boss. It encourages you to pick your battles wisely, as victory could come at a cost. Underhand behavior from others is likely, and someone could try to turn others against you. Be like an eagle and rise above their childish behavior. This isn't a battle worth fighting, and cannot be won. Those who care about you will stand by you. Those who don't have shown you who they are; thank them and walk away.

Six of Swords

KEYWORDS Recuperation, travel, time out, new destinations

The Six of Swords represents the calm after a storm. It often appears following a period of hardship or stress, and heralds the arrival of a calmer cycle in your life. This is a time to leave the drama and arguments to the shows on Netflix, and distance yourself from anything that disrupts your peace. From leaving a stressful job to booking a much-needed vacation, this card signifies the need to put your mental well-being first. Romantically, it can symbolize a period of healing following a break-up or time away from a partner. It can also predict exciting work opportunities overseas, or a journey across water.

Seven of Swords

KEYWORDS Bullying, victimization, disconnection, loss

The Seven of Swords is the Tarot's "thief" card; it can symbolize anything from a co-worker stealing your ideas or taking credit for your work to a needy friend or family member who constantly robs your energy and time. It encourages you to trust your instincts when it comes to others, as there could be a snake around you! Shady behavior from bosses and co-workers can be expected, and a secret shared with a "friend" may be exposed, too. A meddling family member or interfering busybody could test your patience, and a friend or partner's honesty might be questioned as well.

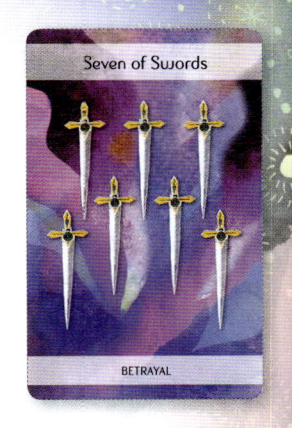

Eight of Swords

KEYWORDS Doorways, newness, adventure, anxiety

The Eight of Swords is a card of restriction. It appears when you're feeling trapped, and your heart is longing to escape whatever is holding you captive. From a job that's paying your bills but crushing your soul to a relationship that's curing your loneliness but making you unhappy, it marks a time when your circumstances are dictating your destiny, and negative thoughts are preventing you from seeing a way out. However, while it may be a card of entrapment, the number eight symbolizes change. So do not give up; learn to control your thoughts, and you'll soon see a way to control your fate.

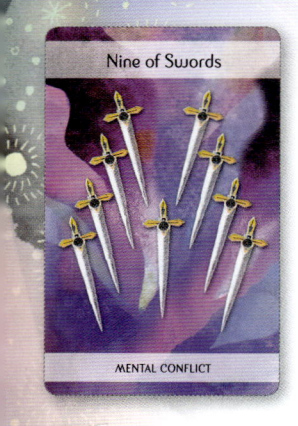

Nine of Swords

KEYWORDS Mindset, fear, anxiety, recuperation

The Nine of Swords symbolizes the "dark night of the soul." It represents a time when your mind becomes your enemy, and negative thoughts follow you around like shadows. Sleepless nights and tearful outbursts are likely, and feelings of guilt, remorse, and regret could invade your mind like a Nordic army. A loved one's distress may also weigh on your shoulders heavily, and the crosses you bear—professionally and personally—could seem too heavy to carry. Pause, breathe, and come back to the present; your anguish may be strong, but the resilience of your spirit is stronger.

Ten of Swords

KEYWORDS Endings, transition, release, freedom

Known as a card of goodbyes, the Ten of Swords marks the end of one era and start of another. Lots of drama can be expected as bridges are burnt and bonds are broken. Events will unfold swiftly and boldly, leaving no room for wishful thinking or doubt. A relationship could end abruptly, or a friend might be in your life one minute, and out of it the next. Betrayals in love, friendships, and work are possible, and a hurtful truth could break your heart, but clear your vision. Look forward rather than back: if it should have been, it would have been; learn from it and move on.

Page of Swords

KEYWORDS Awareness, empowerment, determination, ambition

The Page of Swords is a card of vigilance; it appears when you need to watch what you say—and to whom you say it—as there could be a charlatan around you! It often represents someone who appears sweet and harmless on the outside, but may have a darker side. Like the infamous Nordic squirrel, Ratatoskr, who would run up and down the Tree of Life, stirring up trouble between the eagle at the top and the serpent at the bottom, it suggests someone may try to cause trouble between you and others. Attention to detail is also essential right now, particularly when signing documents or sending emails.

Knight of Swords

KEYWORDS Immaturity, fickleness, ignorance, instability

The Knight of Swords is the troublemaker of the deck; impulsive, reckless, and unpredictable, he causes mayhem wherever he goes, and often lights up your world one minute, and causes a hurricane in it the next! He encourages you to trust what you see, not what you hear, as people's words may not match their actions. Arguments and power struggles with others are likely, and you may discover some shocking truths about someone. A friend or love interest's hot and cold behavior could leave you feeling confused, and there might be some tension in your family as well.

Queen of Swords

KEYWORDS Honesty, sternness, balance, strength

The Queen of Swords is the queen of strength; smart, self-reliant, and full of self-worth, she knows exactly what she wants, and relies on no one but herself to get it. Outspoken, opinionated, and a great judge of character, she often represents a slightly-guarded individual—with a hard outer shell, but soft center—who isn't afraid to speak her mind or stand her ground with others. In a reading, she can symbolize a strong female who will help and empower you. This card can also signify the need to stand up to those around you or establish healthier boundaries with others.

King of Swords

KEYWORDS Knowledge, direction, honesty, stubbornness

The King of Swords rules the mind and intellect; confident, powerful, and a force to be reckoned with, he is fiercely protective of the people he loves, but can seem ruthless, cold, or heartless to those who cross him. Led by his head rather than heart, he often represents a person you respect, such as a parent, partner, or boss, who will shape your future in some way. In a reading, he can predict a new love interest at work or romance with a doctor, lawyer, or military figure. He can also signify the need for logic to overrule emotion in both love and work.